Therefore, my dear brothers and sisters, stand firm. Let nothing move you. Always give yourselves fully to the work of the Lord, because you know that your labor in the Lord is not in vain.

1 Corinthians 15:58

FORWARD:

While we would admit to very few benefits of Covid-19, it has opened up special opportunities to connect with people we wouldn't necessarily have met.

For me, this is how I met Rick Bennett. We both joined the teaching program of Greg Amundson by Zoom connection. Greg put Rick in touch with me, and he's become a regular at our Friday morning Bible study for law enforcement, firefighting and EMT personnel, active and retired.

I've seen Rick's heart for God and his openness as a servant behind the badge. *Send Me* will remind you to be available and prepared before God and community.

These days of extreme stress and uncertainty confront us with God's call and the need to walk into trouble and often danger, representing our Lord through compassion, truth, and hope. *Send Me* will spiritually motivate us to that level.

So we train and prepare for opportunities God calls us too. Allow the words of David to become your prayer. "So be strong and courageous, all you who put your hope in the Lord!" *(Psalm 31.24)*.

Praying and trusting that God will encourage you through *Send Me*.

Dick Johnson, Chaplain
International Conference of Police Chaplains
Santa Cruz, California

MONTH ONE:
SERVICE

Then I heard the Lord asking, "Whom should I send as a messenger to this people? Who will go for us?"

I said, "Here I am. Send me."

Isaiah 6:8
New Living Translation

The prophet Isaiah had a visionary Heavenly wisdom of God's plan, splendor, and glory for us. Even though Isaiah, like all of us, had sinned and fallen short of God's perfect standard, Isaiah models how we should have a fearless willingness to go where God sends us and to complete HIS mission.

As law enforcement, first responders, and military personnel we have the ability to be the messenger for the LORD in a dark world. To take a step up in faith and share God's love, grace, and divine mission to save us through HIS Son Jesus with the people we work with, have contact with, and while we are on duty.

My encouragement to you is to be bold in your faith like Isaiah, and to answer God's calling on your life with HERE I AM LORD. SEND ME!

God blesses those who work for peace, for they will be called the children of God.

Matthew 5:9
New Living Translation

As law enforcement, first responders, and military personnel we are called by our Lord and Savior Christ Jesus to work for peace and resolve in our line of work. However, as we live our lives on and off duty, we are also called to be God's example to those we have contact with in the world of the perfect peace that is only found through God and the salvation and forgiveness of our sins that we have through HIS Son Jesus' sacrifice on the cross.

My encouragement to you today is to be a blessing of peace to those who you have contact with whether you are on or off duty. Shalom.

This is my command—be strong and courageous! Do not be afraid or discouraged. For the Lord your God is with you wherever you go.

Joshua 1:9
New Living Translation

Sometimes in our life, especially as members of the law enforcement, first responder, or military community we find ourselves in an uncontrollable, or unfavorable sideway situation from the calls or operations we are on. These situations are places where difficulty, fear, anxiety, and mental or physical discouragement can fall upon us at anytime, and can possibly follow us even after the call or mission is over. In this Scripture, we are encouraged to be like Joshua, to take courage, and to draw on God's strength instead of our own. We are to have bold confidence that our LORD goes before us everywhere we go and fights with us. Our job is to have faith, trust God's promises for us and be fearless in all we do no matter the odds.

My encouragement for you today is to be like Joshua as we serve the LORD, our communities, and our country. To trust God's Word that is set before us and fearlessly take action by leading through Christ's example.

For you have been called to live in freedom, my brothers and sisters. But don't use your freedom to satisfy your sinful nature. Instead, use your freedom to serve one another in love.

Galatians 5:13
New Living Translation

As Christians and believers in Christ Jesus we have freedom from our sins and have been saved by the grace of God through HIS death and sacrifice on the cross. In a world of constantly being hammered by social media, technology, stress, this new thing or that new thing that we just need to own to make our lives complete, we can easily find ourselves falling back into our old sinful modes of thinking and acting before becoming believers. However, since we are seen as new creations in Christ after believing in HIM and having our sins forgiven, we are called to a higher standard because we have freedom from our sins and we are called to serve one another with love.

My encouragement for today is to look for new and exciting ways to put others first through love, care, and service as Christ would love and care for them.

23 Work willingly at whatever you do, as though you were working for the Lord rather than for people. **24** Remember that the Lord will give you an inheritance as your reward, and that the Master you are serving is Christ.

Colossians 3:23-24
New Living Translation

As members of the law enforcement, first responder, or military community, we have been called to a career of serving others. Whether that be serving our country or the communities we live in, sometimes that role becomes overwhelming with a daily grind of bureaucracy, calls, or the missions or operations that we are assigned. Here we are reminded that as believers in Christ we are working for the LORD and that it is ultimately Christ we are serving instead of the people we serve in our communities, and or even our brothers and sisters that we serve with in our respected agencies.

My encouragement for you today is regardless of the situations that spin up during your time on duty that you willfully work as if Christ is your Chief, Captain, Lieutenant, Sergeant, or any number of people you are in contact with today. Remember your actions will be noticed and you might be the only glimpse of Christ that people see.

Don't copy the behavior and customs of this world, but let God transform you into a new person by changing the way you think. Then you will learn to know God's will for you, which is good and pleasing and perfect.

Romans 12:2
New Living Translation

Living in this world as law enforcement personnel, first responders, or the military community, our actions are constantly a split-second away from being broad-casted over the Internet, or any other media outlet. As we have seen more often than not, those instances that surface that highlight our ill-tempered or sinful actions where we fall short usually tear away from any of the good that we do in our respected fields or agencies. Here Paul reminds us that as believers in Christ we are to set ourselves apart from the world and not to copy or conform to the sin we see in the world.

My encouragement for today is for you to not get caught up with the sinful behavior of this world or the evil that we see out there. To first and foremost through faith in Christ, seek God's pleasing and perfect wisdom in how you conduct yourself whether you are on or off duty. Second, as your faith in Christ grows and transforms you into God's perfect will for your life to model that positive Christ-like example as you serve

13 Be on guard. Stand firm in the faith. Be courageous. Be strong. **14** And do everything with love.

1 Corinthians 16:13-14
New Living Translation

For most of us as law enforcement, first responders, or military personnel, certain phrases are ingrained in us from day one during the academy or basic training like keep your head on a swivel, check your six, and on some level or term keeping the scene safe as threats present themselves. Furthermore, it is pounded into us to work as a team or brotherhood while being "encouraged" to maintain fitness both physically and mentally as we navigate becoming police officers, deputies, EMTs, firefighters, airmen, soldiers, marines, and sailors.

As Christians it is no different than being on a scene or an operation. We need to be alert for the devils' threats and schemes. Not only in our own Christian walk, but also in the walk of our brothers and sisters in Christ. To do this, we must be able to stand firm in God's truth, our foundation of faith in Christ, with fearless strength, mental fitness, and with Christ-like love for one another.

My encouragement for you today is to stand firm in your faith in Christ with everything you do. Continue to seek God's honor and glory in your daily walk with Him through prayer, worship and love.

Whoever pursues righteousness and unfailing love will find life, righteousness, and honor.

Proverbs 21:21
New Living Translation

Most of us called to serve our country in the military, or our communities as law enforcement officers, or as first responders, answered that calling in our lives because we wanted to help people in a crisis, to protect those who needed protection, or to pursue justice for wrongs that were committed against others. Basically to have love for God, family, country, and to do the right thing.

Here we are called by God to pursue and live in righteousness for HIM and have an unfailing love for one another just as Christ loved us. By faith God promises us if we do, that we will be rewarded and find life. Not just life here on Earth, but a spiritual eternal life with HIM in Heaven where we will receive the gift of HIS splendor and glory.

My encouragement for you today is to seek the righteousness of the LORD above all else in your life. The things of this world will fade in time, and all we will have left with is our faith in Christ.

13 "You are the salt of the earth. But what good is salt if it has lost its flavor? Can you make it salty again? It will be thrown out and trampled underfoot as worthless. **14** "You are the light of the world—like a city on a hilltop that cannot be hidden. **15** No one lights a lamp and then puts it under a basket. Instead, a lamp is placed on a stand, where it gives light to everyone in the house. **16** In the same way, let your good deeds shine out for all to see, so that everyone will praise your heavenly Father.

Matthew 5:13-16
New Living Translation

This is one of my favorite Scriptures in the Bible and something that I tell my kids often. It doesn't just apply to law enforcement, first responders, or military personnel, but to every believer in Christ. We are all called to be the salt, an additive to our food to improve its flavor or to preserve it so it doesn't go bad as quickly. We are also called to be a light or a city on the mountainside. That light allows us to see what we could not normally see if we were left standing outside in the dark. Here Christ is calling us to go out into our world that can be a place full of darkness, evil, and rampant with sin, and be the shining example for God's truth to everyone we are in contact with whether we are on or off duty.

My encouragement for you today is for you to be a beacon of hope leading others on a lit path to a life with Christ though your actions.

Don't look out only for your own interests, but take an interest in others, too.

Philippians 2:4
New Living Translation

This briefly sums up in one Scripture why a lot of us got into careers where we serve our country and our communities on a near daily basis. Service is a Christian model of how we are to treat and love others. We are called to pursue Christ's example and to have a servant-like mindset of selflessness and humility and to put others first before our own selfish wants or ambitions.

However, if you notice above, it is good for us to look after our own interests too. The Bible says *"Don't look out ONLY for your own interests."* We have to be able to balance serving others, and taking care of ourselves. If we only seek to serve others, we will not have the mental fitness we need to help take care of or serve others. Likewise, our faith, prayer time, and worship to glorify God has to be growing as well before we can share our faith with others.

My encouragement for you today is to let some of your own unhealthy selfish interests go, and look into ways to turn selfish ambition into acts of selflessness or humility to serve or spread the Gospel with someone you interact with on or off duty.

9 So let's not get tired of doing what is good. At just the right time we will reap a harvest of blessing if we don't give up. **10** Therefore, whenever we have the opportunity, we should do good to everyone—especially to those in the family of faith.

Galatians 6:9-10
New Living Translation

On one level this Scripture describes what happens to a lot of us after we have done the job over and over, year after year. We simply get burnt out and the reasons we got into the career in the first place dries up and we want to give up and quit. However, on another level, it describes another mantra or mental fortitude that a lot of us in the law enforcement, first responder, and military community live by. That mantra is that you are never out of the fight. You embrace the suck and keep going until the job is done.

Our Christian walk works the same way. Sometimes things in our lives get difficult and fall apart, we get tired, we want to give up, we get hung up on past sins, experience the death of someone close, and the list goes on and on and our faith gets attacked. However, we are encouraged here to stay the course and to keep fighting for doing what is good and be looking for ways to be spreading the Gospel message about our LORD and Savior Jesus Christ.

My encouragement to you today is exactly what the Scripture says. Don't get tired of doing what is good. Embrace your faith when life gets difficult on or off duty, and know that God will bless you for not giving up.

God has given each of you a gift from his great variety of spiritual gifts. Use them well to serve one another.

1 Peter 4:10
New Living Translation

What a giving God we serve. God has given us everything that we have in this life including salvation from our sins through HIS Son Jesus. Each of us have additionally been blessed with specific talents or spiritual gifts that God has designed for us to serve HIS purpose. Here Peter is encouraging and calling us to use those talents wisely for God's glory. We are set apart as believers in Christ and called to use those spiritual gifts that we have been blessed with to serve one another to fulfill our purpose as God's people.

My encouragement to you today is to fulfill God's purpose for your life. Use your calling and talents in law enforcement, as an EMT/Paramedic, firefighter, or role in the military to wisely serve one another as we serve our LORD and Savior Jesus.

Search for the Lord and for his strength; continually seek him.

1 Chronicles 16:11
New Living Translation

It seems like we are constantly being torn down by the stresses of this world regardless of our career paths. Add the stresses of the things we see or are faced with on duty as law enforcement, first responders, or military personnel, we can find ourselves overwhelmed in our circumstances. Anxiety and depression can breach our thoughts and push us into a downward spiral if we let it. Here we are encouraged by Ezra to constantly search for the LORD. We are not only to seek God's strength, but also HIS face and favor in our lives. Not just once, but continually.

My encouragement for you today is no matter what difficult challenges or circumstances you faced yesterday, face today, or face tomorrow, there is always strength for us in God and a place for our faith to grow. Seek God everyday in your lives and rest in HIS favor as HIS face shines upon you. Peace be with you.

Work hard so you can present yourself to God and receive his approval. Be a good worker, one who does not need to be ashamed and who correctly explains the word of truth.

2 Timothy 2:15
New Living Translation

Some of the virtues that my Dad instilled in my younger brothers and I when we were growing up were to be honest, hard working, and proud of ourselves for the accomplishments and successes that we received from that hard work. Our spiritual lives are to be no different than our career lives. Regardless of our respected fields, we are to work for the LORD in everything we do. As believers in Christ, we are called to be godly, righteous, holy, and loving towards other people. If we live by that standard, we can be honest and unashamed with how our spiritual life aligns with our physical life.

My encouragement to you is to remember that through Christ's sacrifice on the cross God has made us righteous. Work hard in your respected field and strive to live up to God's standard of approval that has been given to us through our faith in Christ Jesus.

1 Therefore, since we are surrounded by such a huge crowd of witnesses to the life of faith, let us strip off every weight that slows us down, especially the sin that so easily trips us up. And let us run with endurance the race God has set before us. **2** We do this by keeping our eyes on Jesus, the champion who initiates and perfects our faith. Because of the joy awaiting him, he endured the cross, disregarding its shame. Now he is seated in the place of honor beside God's throne.

Hebrews 12:1-2
New Living Translation

With all of the gear and equipment we carry, plus added weight of body armor, weapons, O2 tanks, and other life-saving supplies that some of us carry too, we know what it feels like to have to perform on a scene or operation in our respected fields and feeling weighed down. Sometimes being weighed down can be painful, or cumbersome to our bodies and tough to perform with at an optimum level. Physical endurance is key to do our jobs safely. In our Christian walk, we sometimes feel that same weight that keeps us from performing at our optimum level. The author of Hebrews calls us to remove everything that weighs our faith down, especially the sin in our lives. We do this by confessing our sin, and keeping our focus on Jesus, who perfects our faith as we seek HIM.

My encouragement for you is don't let the things of this world weigh you down. Keep your focus on Christ with persistence and endurance as you grow in your faith.

Fight the good fight for the true faith. Hold tightly to the eternal life to which God has called you, which you have declared so well before many witnesses.

1 Timothy 6:12
New Living Translation

As current or former members of the law enforcement, first responder, and military community, we have answered the calling to serve in the fight for righteousness, justice, and preservation of life. "The Good Fight." However, as believers in Christ, the fight that we are in is a different state of warfare. It is a spiritual fight on a spiritual battlefield. As Christians we are still fighting for righteousness, justice, and preservation of life, however, this fight is a fight of faith with an eternal outcome. To be successful in this warfare, we must seek God's truth in our lives, stand up to and resist evil, and push towards our Heavenly goal and promise of eternal life with our Lord and Savior Christ Jesus.

My encouragement for you today is for you to continue to fight the good fight of true faith with all of Christ's strength. Lean closely into God during times of difficulty, despair, or discouragement, and boldly cling onto God's true promise of eternal life with HIM that only comes through God's grace and our faith in HIS son Jesus.

MONTH ONE: SERVICE

26 For you are all children of God through faith in Christ Jesus.
27 And all who have been united with Christ in baptism have put
on Christ, like putting on new clothes. 28 There is no longer Jew
or Gentile, slave or free, male and female. For you are all one in
Christ Jesus. 29 And now that you belong to Christ, you are the
true children of Abraham. You are his heirs, and God's promise to
Abraham belongs to you.

Galatians 3:26-29
New Living Translation

It is an encouragement to me to know God welcomes me and I am called
HIS child. It means that as believers, through our faith in Christ, we are united
as one body, free from our sins which was made available to each one of us
when we accepted God's free gift of salvation that was made available to
us through Christ's sacrifice on the cross. This is unconditional regardless of
who we are. God says here that those who trust in Christ for salvation are
the full heirs of the LORD and have the rights, privileges, and promises that
come with being HIS true children. We belong to HIM.

My encouragement to you today is to know that God welcomes and loves
you. He sent HIS only son to be a sacrifice for your sins (ref. John 3:16) and
wants to have a personal relationship with you. As our Heavenly Father,
HE desires for you to belong to HIM through placing your faith in Christ
and being in HIS kingdom as one of HIS children.

This Good News tells us how God makes us right in his sight. This is accomplished from start to finish by faith. As the Scriptures say, "It is through faith that a righteous person has life."

Romans 1:17
New Living Translation

The gospel message is a powerful and inspiring illustration of how much God loves us regardless of who we are. We are made right in his sight by our belief and faith in HIS one and only Son Jesus. From the beginning of time when sin entered this world, God's righteousness, mercy, and love for us made it possible for us to be redeemed. Christ's sinless death sacrifice on the cross was the only way our sins could be forgiven. It was the only way we could be saved from the punishment we deserved. Our faith in Christ sets us apart as God's children since God detests sin and can have no part of sin by HIS own nature. HIS grace is what makes it possible for us to have a saving personal relationship with our LORD and Savior Christ Jesus.

My encouragement for you today is if you haven't taken that first step in faith by believing in Christ and the good news of HIS gospel message, do it today. Do not prolong it any longer. Start right now. Pray to our Heavenly Father, ask for forgiveness, and accept HIM as the LORD and Savior of your life. If you are a believer in Christ, my encouragement for you is for you to continue to grow in your faith with Christ everyday. Seek HIM in all that you do. I also hope for everyone reading this right now, that God's grace, mercy, and love will find you wherever you are and fill up inside you. Shalom.

Trust in the Lord with all your heart;
   do not depend on your own understanding.

Proverbs 3:5
New Living Translation

In today's culture, regardless of your respected field, trust can be a hard thing for any one of us to do. I am sure that each one of you can probably think of at least one person in your lifetime who has hurt you in one way or another. Trusting in the Lord can be very hard too because that means we have to give up control of our life, and turn it over to HIM and HIS will for us. The difficulty with that is sometimes our thoughts on what we want to do in life can compete with God's control. The problem with that thinking is we don't know what is best for our lives like God does.

Trusting in God with every ounce of ourselves is a positive and very rewarding paramount duty of our faith. If we truly trust the LORD with all of our heart, then we should not have fear, be afraid, or have any doubts when things hit the fan and we feel the stresses of life. Putting that kind of faith and trust in Christ into our lives replaces our own pride, confidence, and understanding with the confidence, power, and understanding of God.

My encouragement for you today is to open your heart a little more to trusting God. Trust that HE knows what is best for your life, and wants to bless you because of your obedience when you trust in the plan that HE has for you.

MONTH ONE: SERVICE
DAY TWENTY

And I am certain that God, who began the good work within you, will continue his work until it is finally finished on the day when Christ Jesus returns.

Philippians 1:6
New Living Translation

Regardless of your specific respected fields, or what agency you work for, God began a good work in you when you became a believer in Christ. Whether you became a believer years ago or today, our mission is to plug into our faith and grow stronger in faith everyday as long as we are alive on this planet and continue God's work. The career fields we have chosen in our lives movement is paramount for survival. Many of us have heard phases like "get off the X", "get off the train tracks", or "bump up" to describe movement. Either way, you need to MOVE. God wants us to move too. Move in our faith and understanding towards HIM. Christ has blessed each one of us in our careers and career paths. Whether you are in the military, on a medic crew as an EMT or Paramedic, a firefighter, or in a law enforcement agency, you have the ability and the purpose of doing good work for Christ.

My encouragement for you today is regardless of your job, whether you are on duty or off duty, in the United States or abroad, let Christ continue to do HIS good work in you. Continue to "get off the X" and move towards HIM everyday and grow in your faith. HE has begun a good work in you, and still has a lot to do through you. Peace be with you.

God blesses those who hunger and thirst for justice, for they will be satisfied.

Matthew 5:6
New Living Translation

Many of us answered the calling for our lives and entered the military, first responder, and law enforcement career paths to seek justice for others and to make a stand for people in our country and communities that needed our help. Others of us sought to better ourselves, to serve, and make a difference within our lives and what we are doing to benefit our own desires and lives. Here the apostle Matthew challenges us to seek, hunger, and thirst for justice in what we do. However, that justice or righteousness that is spoken about is not how we feel about ourselves or what we have accomplished. Rather, it is more of a challenge to seek and hunger for Christ and HIS will in our lives. It is more about growing in our faith, understanding the blessings of HIS grace and mercy for us, and letting the power of the Holy Spirit make a change in our lives that draws us closer to the LORD. As a result, our relationship with Christ strengthens and we are blessed through HIM.

My encouragement for you today is to continue to turn from your sinful nature and seek the righteousness of the LORD. May God strengthen you and bless you as you hunger for HIS will in your life.

But blessed are those who trust in the Lord
and have made the Lord their hope and confidence.

Jeremiah 17:7
New Living Translation

In our career paths, having trust and confidence in those that we work with is a must. In a lot of our respected fields, the trust and confidence in our fellow brothers and sisters is a matter of safety and their actions could mean the difference between going home safe, or not going home at all. However, how much more awesome are the benefits for those of us that trust in Christ and HIS mission for our lives. Much like trusting in our brothers and sisters who we rely on to keep us safe in a firefight, structure fire, domestic violence scenes, or any number of emergency situations that we might find ourselves in, trusting in God basically and simply means we believe wholeheartedly every word that God has revealed to us through the Holy Scriptures that make up our Holy Bible. When we believe and make Christ our hope and confidence, we expand our faith in and confirm that everything revealed to us through studying HIS word is from God. We are simply applying Heavenly and eternal knowledge of the grace, promises, and blessing of God to our day walk and fellowship in Christ.

My encouragement for you today is that you will continue to put your trust, hope, and confidence in Christ over the things of this world, and that your faith will continue to be blessed and grow abundantly.

MONTH ONE: SERVICE

DAY TWENTY-THREE

So get rid of all the filth and evil in your lives, and humbly accept the word God has planted in your hearts, for it has the power to save your souls.

James 1:21
New Living Translation

In many of our career paths as law enforcement officers, firefighters, EMTs, paramedics, and military personnel stationed stateside or abroad, we see all kinds of filth, darkness, and evil in the people's lives we interact with on a moment by moment basis. We see firsthand how those poor lifestyle choices can affect those people, their families and their children. We also witness the aftermath of hopelessness that comes from those poor decisions.

Our spiritual lives are no different a lot of the time. The only difference is that our filth is often hidden from public view. Many of us have sin that is buried deep, and is literally killing us on all fronts. We need to shed it, and rid ourselves of the weight that sucks us down from being the person that God wants us to be.

Regardless of what sin it is, God detests all sin, and can have no part of it in our lives. James encourages us to accept God's Holy Scripture and to insert it into our lives. To repent and to turn away from the sin in our lives and seek Christ's redemptive power and grace to save us from destruction.

My encouragement for you today is to examine your heart, and ask for Christ to point out anything in your life that is sinful to HIM. Repent of any sin that you have, and seek the power of HIS grace and mercy in your life.

14 So then, since we have a great High Priest who has entered heaven, Jesus the Son of God, let us hold firmly to what we believe. **15** This High Priest of ours understands our weaknesses, for he faced all of the same testings we do, yet he did not sin. **16** So let us come boldly to the throne of our gracious God. There we will receive his mercy, and we will find grace to help us when we need it most.

Hebrews 4:14-16
New Living Translation

Every single one of us, regardless of our choice to join a law enforcement agency, the military, or a career as a firefighter, EMT, or paramedic, has endured struggles, hardships, and trials to get to where you are today. Each one of us had to persevere through our weaknesses to become stronger and build confidence in completing what we were called by God to do. As believers, our spiritual lives have had times where we have endured struggles, hardships, and trials as well. Christ understands our trials, testing, and weaknesses too. HE was tested in every way, but did not sin. As a result, Christ is now exalted at the right hand to God's throne. Through our faith, HE is now our intercessor for the LORD. Through Christ's Heavenly position as the Most High, we now can boldly draw near to our LORD and God when we need HIM the most, and persevere with confidence.

My encouragement for you today is when you feel physically weak or spiritually discouraged, hold a firm grip on your belief and faith in Christ. Boldly seek the LORD, HIS throne and grace in all things.

Now all glory to God, who is able, through his mighty power at work within us, to accomplish infinitely more than we might ask or think.

Ephesians 3:20
New Living Translation

Regardless of our respected occupational paths or the agencies we work for, we train our bodies and minds to exceed the demands of the call, mission, or situation we find ourselves in as we serve. Or at least theoretically we should be training so we will be able to climb to the challenge and push through when we need to dig deep and get business done out in the field.

Our spiritual lives are no different. We need to be able to perform, ask for help when we need it, and train our bodies and our minds for Christ so we can accomplish HIS mission successfully.

In today's scripture, the apostle Paul outlines his desire for us to know with confidence that God is capable of accomplishing more than anything that we can imagine through God's mighty power. The key is found in our faith, and if we are willing to trust in the LORD and to let God's glory work through us or not. If we do, glory will be to our God, our LORD and savior who is able to go above and abundantly do all that we ask or can think of.

My encouragement to you today is give God the glory for everything in your life. Trust in HIS mighty power, seek HIS strength, and let Christ accomplish the great plans HE has for your life.

Therefore, go and make disciples of all the nations, baptizing them in the name of the Father and the Son and the Holy Spirit.

Matthew 28:19
New Living Translation

To many of us, what we do for the agencies we work for is our calling. It is simply built within us to the very core to set ourselves aside and serve others. It is what we live for and our life's mission. As believes in Christ, we have a life's mission too. It is to serve God and to be an example for HIM in everything we do. To share our faith with the people we work with or are in contact with, and to be a light of Godly encouragement in a world full of darkness and despair.

As a Christian living for God, being able to share our faith and lead someone to a saving relationship with our Lord and Savior is our great achievement in life and our mission and calling for the Kingdom or God. One of my greatest honors in life has been being able to share my faith with my two kids, seeing them accept Christ into their lives, and then being able to baptize them. Then watching them grow in faith.

My encouragement to you today is to look for new and exciting ways to encourage others and share your faith with them. Be a shining light.

Don't let evil conquer you, but conquer evil by doing good.

Romans 12:21
New Living Translation

If you really look around our respected agencies, and think about it, you probably can think of at least one of our brothers or sisters that has fallen into a pattern of making poor life choices or has let a destructive lifestyle pattern take a foothold and rule their decisions and life. Unfortunately, we all know or have known people where those events end up conquering them. Those decisions have had negative outcomes that ended up ruining everything they have worked for including their lives, marriages, and careers. As a result, many are left with despair, an overwhelming sense of grief, and hopelessness that has no way out.

The apostle Paul warns and challenges us to not let the evil of sin take a foothold or grip in our lives and destroy us. We can accomplish this by an act of continually seeking Christ's goodness, wisdom, righteousness, grace, and mission in our life. Since Christ conquered the sin of the world through this sacrificial death on the cross and freed us, we as believers need to ask God for forgiveness when we fall short of HIS standard.

My encouragement for you today is to strive to place God's greatness and abounding love for you in your life everyday. Continue to fight the good fight for Christ and seek doing good for HIS Kingdom in everything you do on and off duty.

Since you have been raised to new life with Christ, set your sights on the realities of heaven, where Christ sits in the place of honor at God's right hand.

Colossians 3:1
New Living Translation

As military, law enforcement, and other first responder professionals, many of us have set our sights on our next career move. For a lot of us, the desires of joining an elite special operations group like the Green Berets, Rangers, Marine Recon, SEALS, DEA, the FBI, or your agency's SWAT team could be your focus. For others, the big promotion, advanced training opportunities or certifications to further your career are your main focus as you navigate the ideals of having a successful career. However, as believers in Christ, we are to set our sights vertically higher. When we accept God as our Lord and Savior, we are called to turn from our sinful nature. We have been raised to a new life from our sins through Christ, and HIS sacrifice for us. Since our sins are forgiven, and we are now seen as new beings in Christ through our confession of faith, we need to set our sights and goals on the Heavenly realms and our life with God and serve HIM with honor.

My encouragement to you today is whether you are seeking to join a special operations team, a promotion, or certificate to further your career, seek Christ above all else in your life. Both professionally and personally, set your sights on Heavenly things that are forever over the horizontal world that is just temporary. Shalom.

And it is impossible to please God without faith. Anyone who wants to come to him must believe that God exists and that he rewards those who sincerely seek him.

Hebrews 11:6
New Living Translation

In many of our respected career paths we will find from time to time people and situations where gratitude is expressed for our service to the fields we are embedded in. This gratitude is oftentimes shown by someone buying you a coffee, paying for your breakfast, lunch, or dinner, or just the simple phase "Thank you for your service." These gestures basically say we are pleased with you, your acts of service, and what you stand for. Our Christian walk with God works much in the same way as these gestures. In most cases, our country and the communities we serve have faith and belief in what we do, and we have the reward in serving them and making a difference. To serve God, we have to first say that we believe in God, and believe HE exists. We also have to believe in HIS righteousness and obey HIS instructions found in HIS word. To do this, we have to live by faith since God is now working through us instead of being here on Earth physically. Additionally we need to continue to seek Christ and the reward of Heaven with our whole being by learning more about HIM and HIS desires for us.

My encouragement for you today is take a step for Christ each day. Grow in your faith by seeking HIM in your life and answer HIS calling.

8 God saved you by his grace when you believed. And you can't take credit for this; it is a gift from God. 9 Salvation is not a reward for the good things we have done, so none of us can boast about it. 10 For we are God's masterpiece. He has created us anew in Christ Jesus, so we can do the good things he planned for us long ago.

Ephesians 2:8-10
New Living Translation

The author of Ephesians gives us this perfect example of the awesome power and good news of the gospel message. We are not saved by what we do by our careers or what agency we work for, but only by the free gift of God's grace when we first believed in HIM. None of us deserve salvation from our sins. Instead, because of our sins, we deserve death and destruction because our sinful nature makes us fall short and separates us from the flawlessness of God's righteousness. However, since God created and loves us, HE created a plan through HIS Son Christ Jesus, for us to be renewed and redeemed.

As we finish month one, I want to encourage you and leave you with the spiritual truth that you are God's masterpiece and special to HIM. As a believer in Christ, HIS mercy, grace, and forgiveness of sins made you new and in HIS likeness. God has a plan for your life and serving HIM with everything you have is an instrumental key and blessing. Continue to do the good works that God has blessed you with and planned for you as you serve HIM, your respected agencies, our country, and our communities. Peace be with you in all that you do.

MONTH TWO:
PROTECTION

24 May the Lord bless you and protect you.

25 May the Lord smile on you and be gracious to you.

26 May the Lord show you his favor and give you his peace.

Numbers 6:24-26
New Living Translation

This passage in the Old Testament is a scripture and prayer that my family and I say over each other on a regular basis. We also have it displayed in our home on some of our decor for us to look at as a constant reminder to pray for God's protection, blessing, and peace over us. It is also a prayer that I say every day as I go on patrol and serve my community. Just a quick prayer I say as I go on duty to keep all of us safe as we face the uncertainty of every call we respond to. It is a simple prayer of God's protection and blessing over you and those who serve with you as we face challenges, hostilities, danger, and opposition in a world full of darkness and evil.

My encouragement and prayer for you today is that our LORD and Savior Christ Jesus will bless you, protect you, and be gracious towards you in everything that you do both on and off duty. I hope that God's grace and peace finds you and will be over you always. Shalom.

The Lord is my strength and shield. I trust him with all my heart. He helps me, and my heart is filled with joy. I burst out in songs of thanksgiving.

Psalm 28:7
New Living Translation

In this community and brotherhood of law enforcement, first responders, and military professionals, we oftentimes rely on our own arrogance, strength, training, and actions to get through the day or situation. This way of thinking puts God in our back pocket at best or even at all. On top of this mindset, add in the things that we see and do day in and day out on duty. As a result, we can become full of pride, complacent, numb, and jaded.

In this passage, David sets the example on the warrior mindset. We need to realize who God really is in our lives. He is our foundation and our protector. Additionally, we need to realize that our joy in life comes from the LORD and the LORD only. It is not the money in your bank account, your friends, or the toys we own. More often, we lose sight of this, and get too focused on "me" and "what I'm going though." Here David is claiming who GOD is and setting the example for us of what to be like. We need to trust God for strength and protection with all of our being. To be thankful for what God has done for us, and to be filled with joy that can only come from a relationship with Christ.

My encouragement for today is to be a warrior for God like David. To trust God with everything, and seek HIS strength and joy in your life.

Don't be afraid, for I am with you.
    Don't be discouraged, for I am your God.
I will strengthen you and help you.
    I will hold you up with my victorious right hand.

Isaiah 41:10
New Living Translation

As I face life's challenges whether on or off duty, this scripture is one that
I have committed to memory and pray to God with as I go through the
challenges I am going through. This is a promise from God that HIS grace
will always supply us, protect us, never leave us, and will strengthen us, our
minds, and our hearts. Above everything else, it means that we can trust
HIM in our lives. That HE has us right where HE wants us to be, and we
should not fear or be discouraged with any opposition we face.

My encouragement for you today is to know that God is going to hold
you up with HIS victorious right hand. Trust in HIM and be strengthened.
Do not be afraid or discouraged because HE will help you and never leave
you in the challenges that you are facing.

10 A final word: Be strong in the Lord and in his mighty power. **11** Put on all of God's armor so that you will be able to stand firm against all strategies of the devil. **12** For we are not fighting against flesh-and-blood enemies, but against evil rulers and authorities of the unseen world, against mighty powers in this dark world, and against evil spirits in the heavenly places.**13** Therefore, put on every piece of God's armor so you will be able to resist the enemy in the time of evil. Then after the battle you will still be standing firm.

Ephesians 6:10-13
New Living Translation

As law enforcement, first responder, and military professionals we are all well aware of the dangers of the job we have been called to do. We train physically, mentally, wear protective equipment, and keep our heads on a swivel to make sure we are safe while we do our job. Paul encourages us here first and foremost to be strong in the LORD. Second, for us to put on the full armor of God to protect us from the evil schemes of the Devil and our heavenly spiritual battle against him.

Many of us wear ballistic vests while we are on duty to protect our hearts and vital organs. Physically, our heart keeps us alive. Spiritually speaking, our heart works the same way and where our relationship with God lives. We need to use God's armor to protect our hearts like we use our body armor. Stand firm in your faith, Seek God's truth and resist the evils of sin.

The name of the Lord is a strong fortress; the godly run to him and are safe.

Proverbs 18:10
New Living Translation

As law enforcement, first responders, and military professionals, safety is at the forefront of how we operate on the scenes and missions we go on. Whether it is through operational tactics planning, training, the protective equipment we use, or technology, our main focal objective as we conduct ourselves on duty is to do our job in the safest and best possible way we can. This is not only for our own self preservation or the lives of our brothers and sisters. We do it because we all also want to go home at the end of the day to be with our families, friends, and the people we care for and love in our lives. In a way, our homes, families, and friends are a refuge or "safe place" for our daily lives.

In this short passage of scripture, we are told that God is our strong fortress, and that we need to seek HIM for HIS strength and protection. We can accomplish this through building our faith in Christ and "running" towards HIS righteousness. In doing so, God gives us our peace, joy, and our safety that can only be found through Christ.

My encouragement for you today, is to run to our LORD and Savior Jesus Christ in your life. Build your faith and trust in God above all else and make HIM a strong anchor. Then seek HIS righteousness, strength and protection in your life.

My God is my rock, in whom I find protection. He is my shield, the power that saves me, and my place of safety. He is my refuge, my savior, the one who saves me from violence.

2 Samuel 22:3
New Living Translation

In the current state of our world, we as members of the law enforcement, first responder, and military community see, experience, or are around acts of violence firsthand on a near almost daily level. Unfortunately, each year we are seeing an upward trend of more and more of these acts of violence committed against law enforcement and first responders as we serve our communities. With everything we experience and see on duty, it is easy to become jaded, cynical, and suspicious of people around us. As a result, oftentimes we simply don't trust people or their motives as an act of protecting ourselves. Sometimes, depending on the situation, that mindset is rightfully so. However, the point shared in this passage is that our protection comes from God. Not anywhere else. God protects and shields us from evil, and gives a "safe place" to rest. Not only physically speaking, but emotionally, and spiritually speaking as well. It is through Christ that we are saved from sin. HE is our rock, our shield, our salvation, and our protector.

My encouragement for you today is to trust in the protection of God. Not only physically and mentally, but on a spiritual level too. Seek the shadows of the Lord's protection, and HIS salvation from sin. Take delight in HIM in your life and find joy in Christ Jesus.

1 Those who live in the shelter of the Most High will find rest in the shadow of the Almighty. **2** This I declare about the Lord: He alone is my refuge, my place of safety; he is my God, and I trust him.

Psalm 91:1-2
New Living Translation

One thing about David is he put his hope, trust, and faith in God, and was noted to be a man after God's own heart. David sought a personal relationship with God above all else. He was shielded, protected, and had peace because he put God first and foremost in his life. We as Christians should inspire to be more like David in a lot of ways. Especially striving to be men and women of faith who desire to be people after God's own heart.

My encouragement for you today is to strive to have the faith of David and be a person after God's own heart. Continue to let your faith in Christ grow and place your life under the mighty protection of God. Let the shadow of HIS protection keep you safe and give you peace. Shalom.

I pray that God, the source of hope, will fill you completely with joy and peace because you trust in him. Then you will overflow with confident hope through the power of the Holy Spirit.

Romans 15:13
New Living Translation

In our world today it is evident that there is a lost sense of hope, joy and peace within. We see it all the time in the news, on social media, or calls we are dispatched to. Sadly, we see where sometimes that sense of hopelessness or despair turns overwhelming and someone drastically attempts or accomplishes ending their life. I will tell you right now, if this is you, that regardless of how you feel or what you are going through, God loves you and cares a great deal for you and your life. So much so that he sent HIS only son here to die for your sins and to give you spiritual life. You are important to people and to God. Do not give up!

In our respected career fields, we can become jaded by the hardness of the job and lose hope, joy, and peace in life. This passage however, encourages us when we experience and struggle with this feeling of being jaded or hopeless, we need to boldly pray to God who is our source of hope, joy, and peace with confidence.

The piece of encouragement that I have for you is to constantly seek the hope, joy, and peace that only comes from Christ. I know that real-life struggles exist, and can rob your joy. Therefore, when you feel that struggle, or lack of joy, seek and trust in the LORD with all things.

21 "Submit to God, and you will have peace; then things will go well for you. 22 Listen to his instructions, and store them in your heart.

Job 22:21-22
New Living Translation

If we look even remotely close to what is going on in our world today, we can find people in a state of desperation. Some of it is self-inflicted, some of it is not. If you have ever studied Job, you know that Job was a Godly man. He had wealth and things were going well for him in life. However, the Devil was allowed to take all of it away from him to see if he would remain faithful to the LORD. Even in the middle of the battle, Job had God's peace with him and remained faithful. In the end, God restored and multiplied everything that Job lost.

Sometimes we get discouraged when life seems like things are not going the way they should or when it hits the fan and gets tough. This does not mean that you are no longer under God's protection or blessing. However, oftentimes going through the challenge is the only way our faith can grow. Job was spiritually and physically attacked by Satan and lost everything but his faith. As a result, his faith in God grew. He submitted to God, his faith, and kept God's word at the forefront even under intense pressure.

My encouragement to you is regardless of what is going on in your life today, submit to God and receive HIS wisdom and peace.

But Christ, as the Son, is in charge of God's entire house. And we are God's house, if we keep our courage and remain confident in our hope in Christ.

Hebrews 3:6
New Living Translation

When many accepted the call to join the law enforcement, first responder, or military profession, we did so to join a brotherhood and to take on the role as a servant to our nation and the communities we live in. As followers of Christ, we are in a brotherhood too. A spiritual brotherhood of faith. We are also servants of Christ too as we serve and build the Kingdom of God through loving others, sharing our faith, and worshipping of God our father. Much like when we joined our respected agencies, we took an oath of courage and stepped up to the challenge of wearing the uniform. As believers, we have done the same by taking courage and stepping out by faith, declaring HIM as LORD, clothing ourselves with Christ and making God the leader in our life through our confident hope in HIM. By doing this, we belong to Christ, HIS Heavenly brotherhood that God has placed HIM in charge of, plus make up the body of Christ because HE, as well as the HOLY SPIRIT lives within us.

My encouragement for you today is to be brave and courageous as you continue to pursue your faith in the brotherhood found in Christ Jesus. Let your confidence remain strong, and build you up as your faith grows in trust, hope, and peace of our LORD.

27 Above all, you must live as citizens of heaven, conducting yourselves in a manner worthy of the Good News about Christ. Then, whether I come and see you again or only hear about you, I will know that you are standing together with one spirit and one purpose, fighting together for the faith, which is the Good News. 28 Don't be intimidated in any way by your enemies. This will be a sign to them that they are going to be destroyed, but that you are going to be saved, even by God himself.

Philippians 1:27-28
New Living Translation

One of the reasons I pursued law enforcement was I wanted to serve my community and help make it a safer place to live. I also wanted to make a positive impact on others, as well as be part of something larger than myself. A brotherhood. Many of you joined the military or your respected agencies for the same reasons. As believers in Christ, we are called to a larger mission and a higher standard of conduct. God's mission, God's standard, and God's brotherhood. We stand together, saved by HIS grace in faith as a single brotherhood of brothers and sisters in Christ. Because of Christ's promise and hope of salvation, we should not fear sharing the Good News of God's grace for us. Through Christ, we are protected and set apart as a child of the Most High God. Therefore, go and fight the good fight of faith for God. Spread the Good News of God's love to others and make a positive impact on those you are in contact with.

But in that coming day no weapon turned against you will succeed. You will silence every voice raised up to accuse you. These benefits are enjoyed by the servants of the Lord; their vindication will come from me.

I, the Lord, have spoken!

Isaiah 54:17
New Living Translation

My dad once told me he believed that one of the reasons he made it back home from Vietnam unharmed during the war was because he prayed everyday and made time for the Word of God as often as he could. Many of my friends that have been deployed to Iraq and to Afghanistan over the years have said similar statements as well. All of them had put their hope, trust, and faith in God and that HIS mighty hand was going to guide them, shield them, and protect them from harm while they were serving this country during their combat deployments. God answered their prayers and faithfulness, and they made it home to their families unharmed.

We as believers in Christ have a lot of blessings and benefits of being a Christian besides eternal life with God. One of those added benefits is God's guidance and protection as we serve HIM faithfully.

My encouragement for you today is to seek God's holiness, righteousness, guidance and protection throughout your day. Set time aside to study the Word of God, and reflect on your relationship with Christ. Trust in Christ as HE goes before you leading your steps of faith step by step.

But let all who take refuge in you rejoice; let them sing joyful praises forever. Spread your protection over them, that all who love your name may be filled with joy.

Psalm 5:11
New Living Translation

As men and women who serve our nation and communities as members of law enforcement agencies, first responders, or military personnel, we work in situations and environments that are or can rapidly become dangerous, threatening, hostile, or extremely violent. As a result, we use state-of-the-art protective gear and equipment on the calls or missions we go on. On top of that, we professionally train for these scenarios and situations to help us build tactical skill sets and confidence, so if it happens in the real-world, we can adapt to the threat and mitigate personal injury.

In this passage, David, who had been at war for a long time, encourages and prays for us as believers. As believers in Christ, we are called to have that same bold warrior confidence as David did. We are called to seek the shelter in the LORD above all else and express our love and respect for God through our worship. David's prayer is a prayer of protection over the righteous who love God. It is through our faith, love, and worship of Christ that we express our joy and reverence towards God, thanking HIM for HIS righteousness and everything that HE has done for us.

My encouragement today is to boldly trust that God alone is our rock, our protection and our shield like David did.

Seek the Kingdom of God above all else, and live righteously, and he will give you everything you need.

Matthew 6:33
New Living Translation

All of us started our respected careers on one level or another seeking more in life. For most of us in the field, that "more in life" was more than a paycheck. We wanted to serve on a local or national level, help people in a crisis, fight to bring justice for the wrongs people have committed against others, and the list goes on and on. As believers in Christ, we are called to seek more in our spiritual lives too. We are called to seek and serve God's kingdom above anything else that we might do here on Earth. Additionally, we are called to live by the righteous example that Christ has set for us in the Bible. As we rise to this spiritual standard, our faith and trust builds in Christ. One way we trust in God more is by turning everything over to the LORD. If we do, God promises us in this passage a blessing that he will help us, protect us, and give us everything we need in life.

As you read over Matthew 6:33, my encouragement to you today is to humbly examine yourself before the LORD. Look for new ways to pursue God's Kingdom in your life. This could be developing a set time to pray or devoting a block of time to read the Bible. Additionally, look for things in your life that are holding you down from being the example that Christ has modeled and given to us. Then seek God's wisdom, and strive to a higher standard in your life by building your faith through Christ's righteousness.

10 Fear of the Lord is the foundation of wisdom. Knowledge of the Holy One results in good judgment. **11** Wisdom will multiply your days and add years to your life.

Proverbs 9:10-11
New Living Translation

When we started our careers and went through our agency's hiring process of multiple interviews, polygraph, physiological, and background checks, we were oftentimes asked questions about our character, morals, ethics, and judgment before we were finally hired. Our agencies wanted to make sure that we had the moral fortitude to work for them before we could start the academy, basic training, and work in any capacity for them. As Christians, our fear or the reverence and respect for God and HIS holiness is the basis for our wisdom. As a result, when we seek God through studying the Bible, and trust in Christ and HIS grace for us, we gain good judgment as we conduct ourselves. God's promise to us here is that if we seek HIS wisdom in our lives HE will multiply our days and add years on to our lives.

Unfortunately, we have seen the truth behind this passage in some of the scenes we have been on too. We have seen what happens when people do not make wise choices in life. The horrible aftermaths that result in those choices and who those choices affect are often the saddest.

My encouragement for you today is to seek God's wisdom in life whether you are on or off duty. Be a person of good judgment, moral and ethical fortitude. May God's favor be a blessing on your life each day.

11 All you who fear the Lord, trust the Lord! He is your helper and your shield. 12 The Lord remembers us and will bless us. He will bless the people of Israel and bless the priests, the descendants of Aaron. 13 He will bless those who fear the Lord, both great and lowly.

Psalm 115:11-13
New Living Translation

For all of us there has been one time or another in our careers or just in life in general where we have been afraid. That fear could have been the first time you stepped foot into a structure fire where you knew people were inside. The first high speed pursuit you were in. The first time you tried using stops sticks on a fleeing car rushing down the road at 90 mph at you. The first time you were engaged in a firefight. Or just a time when you had to admit that you screwed up and you didn't know what the outcome was going to be. These are just a few examples of fearful situations we face as we put on the uniform and serve. We also know all too well that this list of fears can go on and on because of the type of work we do.

However, as believers in Christ, we are told to have a different kind of fear. A fear of the LORD. This type of fear is a devout reverence for God. It shows that we have complete trust in the LORD because HE is our helper and our shield. Out of this reverence, God remembers us, and promises us that HE will bless us like he blessed the people of Israel when we have fearful reverence, love, and trust for and in HIM.

My encouragement for you today is to have reverent fear of the LORD and remember that when you put your faith, hope and trust in HIM, HE will help you, shield you, remember you, and bless you.

9 If you make the Lord your refuge, if you make the Most High your shelter, **10** no evil will conquer you; no plague will come near your home. **11** For he will order his angels to protect you wherever you go.

Psalm 91:9-11
New Living Translation

Even though we are part of the community of law enforcement, military, and first responder professionals, at the end of the day we are still human, and have our share of struggles and difficulties like everyone else. Many of you are going through some form of crisis right now as you read this today. Many of you have just finished going through some form of crisis, and some of us are going to be facing some form of crisis in the future. The awesome thing about these verses is it is a promise from God that if we put our trust in HIM, HE will protect us no matter what we are going through. God is described here as a shelter or a place of protection from danger and evil when we put our hope and trust in HIM. We also have the promise that God will offer HIS protection over us wherever we go and keep evil from conquering those who are found in Christ. This is all made possible because of the awesome power and the ultimate sufficiency that Christ endured when HE took our punishment on the cross and died for our sins.

Everywhere we look today, we see the evidence of living in a fallen sinful world. We see pain, suffering, and the result of unholy living on nearly every call. My encouragement for you today is for you to place your faith in the foundational shelter of the LORD, and seek HIS protection in your life daily.

He will protect his faithful ones, but the wicked will disappear in darkness. No one will succeed by strength alone.

1 Samuel 2:9
New Living Translation

When most of us began our careers, our strength was tested and vetted on a daily basis. Even as seasoned members of your respected agencies, your strength is tested by the nature of the work. But as you know, we can not rely on our strength alone to do our jobs or "manhandle" our way through. We have to use positive decision making and exercise morals and ethics to be successful at our jobs too. Unfortunately, we have seen in our agencies, or at least on the news lately, what the repercussions are when our brothers and sisters decide to go against agency policy, or do something immoral, unethical, or illegal. Generally speaking, they disappear from our agencies, go to jail, and they're gone from the brotherhood.

Spiritually speaking, our lives are no different. Through our belief in Christ, the blood that HE shed for us, and HIS death on the cross, we are saved from our sin against God. We are promised through our faith that we will be protected from eternal separation from God. The same remains true if we remain in our sin and rebellion against God. God promises us that we will be cut off from HIM eternally and will be left in darkness. We will simply disappear from HIM and nothing we do by our own doing will prevail against HIM. However, God does not want that for us or any of HIS people. He wants all of us to come to HIM, be redeemed, and saved from eternal darkness. My encouragement for you is to remain faithful to God in your life and be found in HIS light, grace, and mercy.

But those who trust in the Lord will find new strength.
  They will soar high on wings like eagles.
They will run and not grow weary.
  They will walk and not faint.

Isaiah 40:31
New Living Translation

Regardless of the respected agency that you belong to, we have all experienced times where that call, that criminal case, that field training, or that mission wears us down to our very core, and we find ourselves totally exhausted. Our spiritual lives are the same. We can face difficulties, opposition and worldly temptations that challenge our faith, and exhaust us from being the people that God wants us to be. Isaiah reminds us that when we face those challenges in life and in our faith in Christ, that we need to dig deeper and closer to God and HIS word instead of relying on our own strength and resolve. Generally this will just make us more tired and drained by what we are facing. However, if we take the path of Isaiah, and trust in the LORD with what we are facing, we are promised that we will find new strength in God, our faith, and our daily living. This new found strength will help keep us from growing weak or weary in our faith, and will allow for us to excel as the children of God that HE wants us to be.

My encouragement for today is for all of us to remember that God's grace and mercy is sufficient for us no matter the circumstance or difficulty we are facing in life. Trust in the LORD and HIS strength in your life.

18 Having hope will give you courage. You will be protected and will rest in safety. **19** You will lie down unafraid, and many will look to you for help. **20** But the wicked will be blinded. They will have no escape. Their only hope is death."

Job 11:18-20
New Living Translation

Regardless of our respected career paths or what agency we work for, we have all seen people with hope and people without hope at one time or another. Having hope is a powerful mental and physical tool and gives us the power and strength to continue fighting the good fight for our country, our communities, and our lives outside of work. This is especially true when we face opposition and hardship in life both on and off duty. That strength allows for us to take a courageous and confident focus on our jobs, our safety, and our overall mental, emotional, and physical health as we perform in life and at our careers.

Our faith works in the same way. As believers in Christ, we have the hope of salvation that is found through our relationship with Christ and HIS sacrifice on the cross for us. That faith based hope gives us strength when our faith gets rattled a little in life. It allows for us to persevere through hardships like Job did, and know with bold confidence that God loves us and will protect us as HIS children. It also allows for us to be a shining light and a voice for Christ to others that have gone through, or are going through the same thing we have as believers.

Have fearless faith and fight the good fight for Christ today. Shalom.

Turn your ear to listen to me; rescue me quickly. Be my rock of protection, a fortress where I will be safe.

Psalm 31:2
New Living Translation

When we get dispatched to a frantic scene or sent on a hot mission and things go sideways for us in a bad way, we want backup or help from our brothers and sisters. Whether that be additional manpower, equipment, or aerial fire support, we want people to know we need help in that hostile or crisis situation. Preferably with as fast as possible results so we can regain some level of safety, cover of protection, and control of what is going on in that particular situation.

As followers of Christ, we communicate with God through our prayers and spending time seeking HIM. We should want and desire for God to hear us, be with us, and protect us in any situation we are going through in life. We should want God to lead the way for us and to be our additional manpower and hedge of protection when life goes sideways. This comes from trusting and giving control of our lives over to God like David. With that trust in the LORD, we should also pray with confidence to God like David did. In this passage, David is praying for God to shine HIS face on him and to listen to his prayers. To deliver him from his opposition, and to be his shelter, protection and foundation.

My hope for you today is for your faith to grow closer to God. Seek God like David did, and be a person of faith after God's own heart in your life. I pray that Christ's protection will surround you and keep you safe.

3 You will keep in perfect peace all who trust in you, all whose thoughts are fixed on you! 4 Trust in the Lord always, for the Lord God is the eternal Rock.

Isaiah 26:3-4
New Living Translation

For many of us, we started careers in law enforcement and the military because we wanted to fight for righteousness, peace, and the protection of others. Regardless of why you answered the call to serve, we all did, and are now called to a higher purpose to be peacemakers. Deep down in each of us, *"To Serve and Protect"* is a character trait we all share and is something we strive to do. That virtue is also one of the iconic graphics and mottoes found on the majority of our law enforcement patrol units across this nation. A virtue that serves as a key reminder of trust and our commitment to our agencies, our communities and our nation.

As believers, we have made a commitment too. A commitment to God and to put our faith and trust in HIS son Jesus Christ. HE is our peacemaker, our savior, our eternal rock, and our unshakable foundation to hold on to for hope and protection. Isaiah reminds us to always put our trust in God regardless of the hardships happening in life. We need to seek to live in God's perfect peace found only through our faith and salvation in Christ.

My encouragement for you today is to seek to align yourselves with God's peace and protection. Be a peacemaker with a moral character virtue and motto *"To Serve God, and Seek HIS Protection."*

"God's way is perfect. All the Lord's promises prove true. He is a shield for all who look to him for protection.

2 Samuel 22:31
New Living Translation

For many of us, we wear a badge on our uniforms everyday when we go to work. That metal badge is a symbol that represents our commitment to protect our communities, to be ambassadors for our agencies, and to hold ourselves to a higher moral and ethical standard. Unfortunately, time and time again we have seen in the news or on social media where one of our brothers or sisters has fallen short of the standards or responsibility that comes with wearing the badge.

As believers in Christ, we wear a badge that is representative of our faith in God. That shield of faith is a symbol of Christ's love for us, and it provides us with an example of God's perfect and flawless standard that HE set for us in HIS word. When we stepped out in Christian faith, we admitted that we have fallen short of the standards that come with wearing the God's badge and that we needed Christ's forgiveness in our lives. With Christ in our lives, we need to physically and spiritually seek and look towards God for HIS leadership and protection in our lives.

My encouragement for you today is to trust in God's perfect and flawless will for your life as you step out and grow in your faith. Continue to wrap yourself with HIS shield, and lean into HIS physical and spiritual hedge of protection daily.

10 Many sorrows come to the wicked, but unfailing love surrounds those who trust the Lord. **11** So rejoice in the Lord and be glad, all you who obey him! Shout for joy, all you whose hearts are pure!

Psalm 32:10-11
New Living Translation

Regardless of what agency or military branch you are in, all of us in this field of work have seen where people's wickedness takes them on one level or another. We don't even have to look very far in our communities, and we can see people's lives shattered by the choices they have made. Not to mention the downward spiral of destruction or the adverse ripple effects that send out like shock waves. The pastors at the church my family and I attend have ingrained in my kids at youth group, and the rest of the church for that matter, the coined phrase "you show me your friends, and I will show you your future." There is a lot of truth in that statement. Our wickedness and sin follows us everywhere we go when we stay in our rebellion. It also keeps us from being the people God wants us to be on or off duty, and anywhere we go in between. However, even though Christ loved us, and died for our sins when we were still sinners, when we turn from the sinful rebellion in our life, God's love encompasses us and blesses us. Therefore, because of our salvation and forgiveness found in Christ, we should be excited and praise God in everything we do.

My encouragement for you today is to seek out any sin in your life and ask for God to forgive you of it. Choose to trust and obey God in your life.

The Lord himself will fight for you. Just stay calm.

Exodus 14:14
New Living Translation

I remember when I started in law enforcement as a reserve deputy sheriff being told to relax, breathe, and slow down when we were going through our firearms training block in the academy. This training was ingrained in us because we train like we fight, and our instructors wanted us to have a solid training building block of staying calm in situations when things were hitting the fan for real and lives could be at stake. When we go on a hot call, hectic scene, or a high-level mission, many times when we arrive, we find ourselves in the middle of chaos. It could be easy to get overwhelmed if we don't focus on our job and what we need to do. Having a calm demeanor allows for us to think clearly and focus on what we need to focus on.

Our spiritual lives are the same way. We need to train like we fight spiritually. There are a lot of times in our lives where we need to relax, breathe, and slow down in the middle of one of the life's hardships or ambushes we find ourselves going through. This passage reminds us as believers in Christ that God goes before us and fights for us on both a physical and spiritual level. We just have to breathe, trust God, and stay calm.

My encouragement for you today is remember that we train like we fight. Continue to seek God's will for your life and trust the LORD's promise to us that HE goes before us and fights for us. Our job is to stay calm and let God breathe through us.

16 But whenever someone turns to the Lord, the veil is taken away.
17 For the Lord is the Spirit, and wherever the Spirit of the Lord is,
there is freedom. 18 So all of us who have had that veil removed
can see and reflect the glory of the Lord. And the Lord—who is the
Spirit—makes us more and more like him as we are changed into his
glorious image.

2 Corinthians 3:16-18
New Living Translation

Your ability to see clearly physically and mentally in this job field is a key
component. Your vision keeps you focused, and honed in from overlooking
important factors that could protect you from harmful situations and or save
your life. Likewise the lack of vision works in the reverse order. Everything is
fuzzy or not clear, and we can find ourselves stumbling to make it out. Sin
in our lives works the same way. Sin clouds our judgment, jams us up, and
keeps us from seeing what God wants for us. When we remove the sin in
our lives, that fuzziness goes away and we can see God's righteousness and
desire for us as HIS children.

My encouragement for you today is to free yourself from any sin that
you have in your life. Clearly look towards Christ's example in your life and
focus on HIS perfect will for you. Finally, seek, reflect, and praise God for
HIS glory, righteousness, and physical and spiritual protection.

6 Don't worry about anything; instead, pray about everything. Tell God what you need, and thank him for all he has done. 7 Then you will experience God's peace, which exceeds anything we can understand. His peace will guard your hearts and minds as you live in Christ Jesus.

Philippians 4:6-7
New Living Translation

Regardless of the respected agency you work for or the community you reside in, we all live and go through stressful times. Whether you are on or off duty, or deployed to another country, what we see and do in the field can be physically, mentally, and emotionally draining. Not to mention any added pressures of our lives at home. With everything mounting on us daily, it is extremely easy to stress out or worry when things hit the fan. Unfortunately, and all to often, that stress leads to unhealthy lifestyles, which can include drinking to much, unhealthy eating, not exercising, confiding in or hanging out too much with coworkers of the opposite sex who are not our spouses. The list of physical and spiritual negatives go on and on. However, God does not want us to worry about anything. HE wants us to give our stresses and concerns over to HIM, to trust in HIS understanding, and let HIM fight our battles for us. If we do, HE promises here to protect our hearts and minds, and give us peace as we live in Christ.

I know life can mount up and get crazy. My advice for the day is in those situations, keep calm, and give that stress to Christ. Let HIM work through it and fight your battle, and give you peace. Shalom.

And I am convinced that nothing can ever separate us from God's love. Neither death nor life, neither angels nor demons, neither our fears for today nor our worries about tomorrow—not even the powers of hell can separate us from God's love.

Romans 8:38
New Living Translation

In our society today, the word "Love" has lost a lot of its meaning. It is a word that is now thrown around loosely with empty meaning to describe stuff we own. For instance, we will say we "Love" our house, but will move to a newer, nicer, bigger one when we see one we like for a good price. We say we "Love" our car, but will trade it in on a newer model as soon as we can. We will say we "Love" our spouse or significant other, but oftentimes don't treat them like the loving person we should. Or worse, when things get rough, or hit the fan, there is a split and a family is divided. The reality is, our thoughts on what "Love" is can be pretty shallow at times.

God's love is never shallow. It is whole-hearted and does not contain ulterior motives. Additionally, the love that the LORD has for us is a proven true love that will never leave or fail. God proved HIS love for us by giving us HIS only son Jesus to pay for our sin once and for all. That is that kind of love that can only be found through HIS supreme righteousness, grace, mercy, and the desire that HE has to have a real relationship with us.

My encouragement for you today is trust in the power of God's love for you and your life. Apply that love to your faith in HIM, and look for new ways to show and spread God's love throughout your community as you serve.

1 In that day you will sing: "I will praise you, O Lord! You were angry with me, but not any more. Now you comfort me. **2** See, God has come to save me. I will trust in him and not be afraid. The Lord God is my strength and my song; he has given me victory."

Isaiah 12:1-2
New Living Translation

When we joined our respected agencies, we made a commitment to serve, to protect, and to fight for justice and righteousness in our nation and our communities. To do so, we swore an oath to live by a warrior's mindset of fearlessness, strength, and honor. The prophet Isaiah had a warrior's faith for the LORD and led others by his Godly example. He took courage, praised God, trusted God, asked God for forgiveness, and then applied God's divine wisdom to his life as he served and fought for the LORD.

As believers in Christ, we need to have the same warrior mindset and patriotism for God as we do for our nation and the communities we serve. Just like Isaiah, we need to lead the people we interact with, whether on or off duty, by our Christian faith. We can do this the same way Isaiah did, through our humility, courage, strength, and honor we have for Christ.

My encouragement for you today is to take a step in faith like Isaiah. Praise God often. Seek God's truth, comfort, protection, and forgiveness in your life. Then lead others by an example of faith with your walk with Christ.

3 Death wrapped its ropes around me; the terrors of the grave over took me. I saw only trouble and sorrow. 4 Then I called on the name of the Lord: "Please, Lord, save me!" 5 How kind the Lord is! How good he is! So merciful, this God of ours! 6 The Lord protects those of childlike faith; I was facing death, and he saved me.

Psalm 116:3-6
New Living Translation

King David is described as an incredible warrior, a person full of wisdom and wealth, and a man with a heart and devotion for the LORD. However, there were times in his life where trouble, adversity, and sin followed him. For instance when he was living on the run because King Saul wanted to kill him or when he had an affair with Bathsheba and had her husband killed in battle to cover it up after she became pregnant.

Our lives are no different than David's life in many ways. Unfortunately, in the world we live in today, there are people that want to kill us because of our occupations, the country we live in, and/or because of our faith in Christ. Second, all of us have also sinned against God in one way or another, and need HIS salvation. Third, Christ can use us, and our mistakes, to further God's Kingdom for HIS glory and honor. David understood these things both on a physical level and on a spiritual level and reached out in faith to the LORD for help. As physical and spiritual warriors, we need to be like David and realize we need God's presence in our lives. We need to search for God's divine purpose, forgiveness, and physical and spiritual protection with the faith of an innocent child in everything we do. May the peace and protection of the LORD be with you today.

MONTH THREE:
STRENGTH

These trials will show that your faith is genuine. It is being tested as fire tests and purifies gold—though your faith is far more precious than mere gold. So when your faith remains strong through many trials, it will bring you much praise and glory and honor on the day when Jesus Christ is revealed to the whole world.

1 Peter 1:7
New Living Translation

When we started our careers, we were all tested, vetted, and had our limits pushed to prove that we were capable of doing the job. After we successfully completed our training, we graduated, and started the process of working and furthering our careers. By being tested, we have shown our agencies that we had the strength to do so, and that we had grit, determination, and were serious about the work we do.

Our faith can be tested in the same way we were tested in our agency academies or military training. Sometimes our spiritual and physical lives get rough and we have to push harder, dig deeper, carry on further, and just not give up or quit. When we persevere in our faith, our spiritual lives build strength, grow, and are refined. That refining allows for us to bring praise, honor, and glory to Christ through our faith and persistence. It also gives us the ability to be used by GOD, and share our faith or story with others that are going through the challenges that we are facing or have faced in the past.

My encouragement to you today is to grow stronger in the LORD when you face challenges. Even though it might be difficult and painful now, like the pain we endured going through our field training, the reward in our faith is far greater when we push through and succeed.

For you know that when your faith is tested, your endurance has a chance to grow.

James 1:3
New Living Translation

Every single one of us that has even spent a short amount of time working in law enforcement, as a first responder, or as a member of our armed forces knows that this job tests our endurance on a daily basis through the stresses we face on and off duty. We can combat some of that stress by training and growing physically and mentally stronger as we gain experience in the field. This allows us to build more stamina and the ability to operate in the harsh conditions that we face on the calls, scenes, and missions we are involved in.

In many ways our Christian faith works in the same manner. Every single one of us has been through difficult times, a crisis, a trial, or some kind of life ambush that derails us to the core. Sometimes, those instances bring out the worst in us, tear us down, and knock us out of the fight. That is what the Devil wants. He wants to do nothing more other than to kill us, steal us from God, and to destroy us from being the men and women that Christ has called us to be for HIS kingdom. However, when we seek God in those challenging times, even though we might be knocked down hard, we have an opportunity to grow in our faith and build our faith to a higher level. When our faith grows in Christ, it gives us the ability to endure more when we find ourselves experiencing hard times. It also gives us a unique opportunity to share our faith and our real-life struggles with others, and be an example of faith for Christ.

My encouragement today is even though things might be tough going for you now, lean on Christ more than ever. Keep fighting, and be the person of faith that God is calling you to be.

He renews my strength. He guides me along right paths, bringing honor to his name.

Psalm 23:3
New Living Translation

Oftentimes in this line of work, we get dispatched to call with the potential of it being a hostile scene, or we can be sent on a high-level target mission to get some really bad people. When we go on these types of operations, most agencies will take time to stage off-site prior to going in for a final Intel briefing and will have a formulated plan that will set us up for a successful raid and relatively safe operation. To be successful, we all need to be on the same level when conducting the operation, and we need to know what needs to be done, and what tasks are expected of each of us during the op. Essentially, we all need to be on the same page at the same time.

In many ways our walk with Christ works along the same lines of preparing for an operation in the field. When we set time aside out of our day to spend time with God through prayer and reading the Bible, we are for all intents and purposes attending an Intel briefing of faith with God. That "Intel briefing" is an off-site Heavenly staging area that aligns our lives with Christ, which puts us on the same page with HIM. This allows for God to guide us down the right and narrow path. A path towards HIS righteousness and will for our lives. When we are on that path with God, our faith is renewed and strengthened and we bring glory to HIS name.

My encouragement to you today is set some time aside and stage an Intel briefing with God. May your life in Christ be renewed and strengthened.

So be strong and courageous! Do not be afraid and do not panic
before them. For the Lord your God will personally go ahead of you.
He will neither fail you nor abandon you.

Deuteronomy 31:6
New Living Translation

As members of a law enforcement, first responder, or military community all
of us have gone on a call or mission where we had an adrenaline spike of
fear go through us. It is natural regardless of who we are.

When we became believers in Christ, God supplied us with the Holy Spirit
to help guide us in our faith. As the Holy Spirit lives in us and guides us, HE
also challenges us to be strong in the Lord in all things of our lives. This is
especially true when we face opposition, difficult situations, and the life
ambushes that come from nowhere. During these uncertain times, we need
to remember that God will not fail us or leave us high and dry. The outcome
of the situation might not be what we thought it would be, but God knows
what is best for us. Plus, it usually gives us an opportunity to grow in our
faith and give us a voice to encourage someone else. We additionally
need to remember that we have put our trust in Christ, and HE has it under
control. This is because HE goes before us and has already gone through
what we are going though. Our job is to remain confident, strong, and
courageous while Christ works before us and in us.

My encouragement to you today be bold, strong, and courageous. Not
only in our careers, but also in your faith with Christ. Live fearlessly because
God goes before you in all things.

Patient endurance is what you need now, so that you will continue to do God's will. Then you will receive all that he has promised.

Hebrews 10:36
New Living Translation

Probably one of the hardest things to do in life is being patient. We live in a society where we want things now, easier, and to go faster than ever before. Our careers are no different than our home lives either. We want the "bad people" we encounter to face justice now. We want specific advancement opportunities now, to be accepted in special units, task forces, or elite groups now, or maybe just a big promotion to make more money now. Either way when we really look at it, most of us don't want to wait and can be greedy, selfish, and mean about getting what we want. We want it all right now. The really sad thing is our lists of what we want grows daily and goes on and on because of our failure to be content. The more things we have on that list, the more our behavior can be uglier to get them. I am just as guilty as the next person on this too. It is just so easy to get distracted by all of the stuff we see in this world, and down the rabbit hole we go.

However, as believers in Christ, we need to have spiritual and physical patience in our lives. Having patience in our spiritual walk with Christ keeps us focused on doing what God's will is for our lives, allowing for us to be grounded in Christ. Which sometimes is really tough, because we want God to answer us right now just like we want our "new something" on our list right now. Listening to God and waiting on HIM makes us grow in our faith. It makes us give up our control, and rely on God's timing instead of our own. All of which brings honor and glory to HIS name and kingdom.

For I can do everything through Christ, who gives me strength.

Philippians 4:13
New Living Translation

If you look around, it does not take very long to see suffering and pain in the lives of the people around us. On duty or off duty, we see it everyday. Some of you are going through your very own suffering as you read this. Life can be an all out fist fight sometimes, and it sucks. This scripture is one of my Father-in-law's favorites verses in the Bible because it helped him go through an extremely difficult time in his life. A time in his life of suffering the horrible pain of the "tank", skin graft surgeries, and intensive rehabilitation after being burnt over 60 percent of his body in a double gas explosion at work. During his recovery, he committed this verse to help him get through the next round of pain, the next round of surgeries, and the next round of rehab.

As followers in Christ, Paul is encouraging us about how to deal with our suffering and life ambushes. If you read more in this section of Philippians, you will see that he was in need and suffering. However, instead of pointing his suffering out to us, Paul sets an example for us on how to deal with our pain and suffering by proclaiming that his strength doesn't come from figuring out how to get through his situation. Instead, all of his strength comes from having Christ in his life. And because of that, he can accomplish what God's will is for him. Just like how my Father-in-law used God's strength to get through his long and extensive recovery.

My encouragement for you today is no matter what your struggles are, lean on Christ now, and let God strengthen you and help you overcome.

MONTH THREE: STRENGTH
DAY SEVEN

For God has not given us a spirit of fear and timidity, but of power, love, and self-discipline.

2 Timothy 1:7
New Living Translation

When we took it upon ourselves and answered the call to serve, we took on the honor and responsibility of wearing the uniform. Regardless of the agency, station, or military branch we are attached to, we were all disciplined and vetted through our training to make us the men and women that we are today. That discipline builds us up and gives us confidence, strength, and mental fortitude to respond to the times when we face opposition, hostility, and potentially life-threatening situations in the world in which we work and operate. Our confidence in these situations gives us the strength and the determination we need to operate fearlessly with power to do what we need to do to on any call, operation, or mission.

Our walk with Christ works the same way. When we became believers in Christ, we made a stand for God, and answered HIS calling for our lives as Christians. When we professed our faith, we received God's Holy Spirit. HE helps guide us through a dark ungodly world that is full of opposition and hostility. With Christ's Spirit, we do not need to live in fear and can now go fearlessly into this world with love for all of HIS people and be a shining light for God's Kingdom though our love and service to Christ.

My word of encouragement for you today is don't be timid about your faith in Christ. Be the roaring lion that you are called to be for God, and live a life full of love, strength and self-control for the LORD.

17 Then Christ will make his home in your hearts as you trust in him. Your roots will grow down into God's love and keep you strong. **18** And may you have the power to understand, as all God's people should, how wide, how long, how high, and how deep his love is.

Ephesians 3:17-18
New Living Translation

There are many of us out there that live in our mistakes, our sins, and our shame daily, and seem to not be able to move past them. Our past mistakes, and things we have seen or done on duty can literally haunt us and eat us alive. While it is true that we have all sinned and have fallen short of God's perfect standard, we have a redeemer, Jesus Christ. Unfortunately, some of us can not accept that either, and continue to live in our depression, despair, and sinful ways. Often times our past gives us false perceptions that we are too bad of a person to go to God, or that we have done something that can not be forgiven, or that we don't deserve God's love in the first place. These thoughts are simply untrue and are lies from the Devil.

These scriptures from Paul sum up how God really feels about us. That encouragement alone should strengthen us. When we accepted Christ in our life, HE took up a residence in us. Our bodies then became a temple or dwelling place for the LORD. As we take up our faith in Christ through our studying of the Bible, reading devotionals, attending church, and praying, we build a stronger foundation and understanding of God's desire and love for us. Paul also encourages us by explaining how deep God's love is for us regardless of our past. God's love for you reaches farther and deeper than you can even imagine. Remember HIS only son, Jesus, died for you.

My old self has been crucified with Christ. It is no longer I who live, but Christ lives in me. So I live in this earthly body by trusting in the Son of God, who loved me and gave himself for me.

Galatians 2:20
New Living Translation

When we were sworn in, we swore an oath we must uphold in our communities, our state, and to our nation. That oath sets us apart from the people that are not in law enforcement, fire, rescue, para-medicine or the military because of our commitment to our communities and our nation. That oath also set us on a path to live by a higher standard of conduct which comes with a great deal of responsibility.

When we accepted Christ in our lives, we set ourselves apart from the men and women we used to be when we declared Christ as LORD of our lives. When we made our declaration of faith as followers of Christ, we acknowledged that we were sinners, and that we needed God in our lives. By doing this, we have now died from our old ways just like Christ died for us when HE was crucified on the cross. This means we should no longer be living for our own gratification and sinful desires, but living for Christ and for God's righteousness in our lives because Christ gave HIMSELF as a ransom for our sins.

My encouragement for you today is to completely trust in the LORD with all of your soul and strength. Give one hundred percent of yourself to Christ. HE loves you, died for you, and lives within you. May Christ strengthen you today.

MONTH THREE: STRENGTH

DAY TEN

14 Work at living in peace with everyone, and work at living a holy life, for those who are not holy will not see the Lord. **15** Look after each other so that none of you fails to receive the grace of God. Watch out that no poisonous root of bitterness grows up to trouble you, corrupting many.

Hebrews 12:14-15
New Living Translation

When it gets down to the basics, this scripture is why a lot of us got into the professions that we did. Of course, we probably did not think of this passage when we went into law enforcement, fire, rescue, para-medicine, or the military. However, for the most part all of us joined our agencies or branches because we were called to perform a civic duty, and wanted to make a positive difference in the lives of other people, while helping our nation and our communities be better and safer places to live.

   As followers of Christ, we have been called to perform a civic duty for God and HIS Kingdom. Therefore, we need to strive to live a higher moral and ethical standard than what we normally do on duty. We need lose any bias or animosity we have between us and other people. This is so we can continue to work for the LORD, HIS righteousness, and be an example for HIS grace, mercy, and peace to others. If we do this, others may see God's holiness in us. Additionally, just like when we are on a call, scene, or op and we must watch our brothers' and sisters' six, the same also applies to us as believers. We are called to watch over and protect our Christian brothers and sisters to help them grow and succeed in their faith, and to encourage them and strengthen them through God.

God arms me with strength,
 and he makes my way perfect.

Psalm 18:32
New Living Translation

If you look across our communities today, we see the effects of people trying to rely solely on themselves for their success. Sometimes this has positive effects, and other times this has negative effects. The problem that can develop out of this thinking is a tendency to become greedy and selfish, which puts God in our back pocket.

The point that David is encouraging us with here is that as believers, our strength should not come from ourselves, but instead it should come from Christ. God inspires us with HIS guidance, courage, and mental resolve. In addition, HE gives us the physical and mental strength that prepares us for the battles we face in our lives and in our faith. Furthermore, just like every single one of us, David was not a perfect person. He fell short of God's perfect standard just like we do. However, David acknowledged his flaws often, repented of his failures, and chose to keep focused on following after God's righteousness which kept him on the same path with God.

My encouragement for you today is to arm yourself and your faith with God's strength. Acknowledged your flaws like David, and repented of your failures. Continue to pursue after God's righteousness in your life which will lead you on HIS perfect path.

MONTH THREE: STRENGTH

Fear of the Lord is the foundation of true knowledge,
but fools despise wisdom and discipline.

Proverbs 1:7
New Living Translation

From the very beginning and throughout the length of our careers we have gone to repeated trainings to give us more knowledge and to help make us more effective at our jobs and in our respected agencies. That continuous training of mind and body has allowed for us to be discipled in a true wisdom that makes us effective warriors for our communities and nation. We have also all seen the reverse of this thought process and the aftershocks and ripple effects that follow poor decision making. Unfortunately, this happens within the agencies we are attached to, and the communities we serve.

As believers in Christ, when we put all of our hope and trust the in the LORD, study the Bible, fellowship with other believers, and attend church and Bible studies, we are laying positive ground work like we do on the job to make us better and more effective public servants. This is what King Solomon is referring to here is Proverbs. It is not that we are afraid or fearful of God. Rather, we are in awe of God's awesomeness, with complete reverence for HIM and HIS grace for us. This reverence for Christ strengthens us and helps us build a solid foundation of faith that is based on God's true knowledge, mercy, and love for HIS children.

My encouragement for you today is make God the foundation of your life and trust in HIS knowledge and will for you. Accept, devote, and strengthen yourself in the wisdom and discipline that comes only from Christ. Shalom.

But as for you, be strong and courageous,
for your work will be rewarded.

2 Chronicles 15:7
New Living Translation

We have all entered into careers of service, and face situations everyday in which we must be courageous and strong both mentally and physically. People's lives can literally hang in a 50/50 balance based on how we perform our jobs. It can be extremely tough going especially if we are bouncing from call to call, operation to operation day in, and day out. This high-stakes atmosphere can beat us down and devour a person, mentally, emotionally, and physically. This could be one of the reasons we are seeing such an alarming rate of burnout and suicide in our respected fields. We feel ground up and see no relief in what we are facing. If this is you, my encouragement is to talk with someone about it today. It could be a close friend, family member, co-worker, pastor, department chaplain, or a counselor. Get what you are struggling with out in the open. I know that this can be extremely hard, but doing so, will help clear your mind and start the healing process.

As believers in Christ, we have real struggles in life too, and we have to be courageous and strong mentally and physically just like we do on duty. The difference is our spiritual life is at stake. This is why it is so important to keep ourselves grounded in our faith and in the LORD. My take away from today's passage is boldly draw closer to Christ each day and be strengthened by HIM. Studying the Bible, pray, talk with other believers, and seek God's divine will for your life in everything you do. Be rewarded and blessed today.

3 We can rejoice, too, when we run into problems and trials, for we know that they help us develop endurance. 4 And endurance develops strength of character, and character strengthens our confident hope of salvation.

Romans 5:3-4
New Living Translation

Regardless of the agency you work for, we have all been jammed up by challenges, conflicts, and struggles on the job. Not to mention what occurs in our own personal lives. Every year seems challenging, but the year of 2020 seemed to wear people thin professionally and personally. We saw a push to defund the police, massive riots, COVID, and divisions between people in this country like we have never seen before, and an overarching theme of negativity.

However in Romans, Paul encourages us to be strengthened in those times in our lives when we encounter life ambushes, or situations simply hit the fan in life and don't go the way we expected. When we are strengthened through those experiences, we develop endurance, much like when we started our careers, and we were physically pushed in our basic academy or basic training. That endurance, made us stronger mentally and physically, and built our confidence and character to do our jobs. When our faith encounters these times, we have an opportunity to push through like we did in PT. The difference is we build faith-based endurance, and character. This can be used to strengthened our salvation in Christ, and to share the gospel with people that we meet throughout our lives.

5 In view of all this, make every effort to respond to God's promises. Supplement your faith with a generous provision of moral excellence, and moral excellence with knowledge, **6** and knowledge with self-control, and self-control with patient endurance, and patient endurance with godliness, **7** and godliness with brotherly affection, and brotherly affection with love for everyone.

2 Peter 1:5-7
New Living Translation

When you joined your agency or military branch, one of the first things you were given and promised to live by was a moral creed or values for your agency, department, or branch of service. These creeds are not just words on a page, but the life-blood of how we should conduct ourselves as men and women that wear the uniform.

As followers of Christ, we have a moral creed that we have responded to as well. When we became believers, we made our creed with God. We proclaimed HIS truth, and made it the backbone of our Christian faith. What does that really mean though? Peter outlines how we should conduct ourselves as Christian men and women today. We need to live a life of committing ourselves to God's righteousness and moral excellence. We need to have a hunger for knowing God more each day and desiring HIS will for our lives. We need to be people with self-control and patience. We also need to have a Godly love for other people regardless of who they are.

My take away for today, is to commit each of these characteristics to your daily life and walk with Christ. Build upon them, and strengthen yourself and your faith in every effort to respond to God's promises and affection for you.

May the Lord lead your hearts into a full understanding and expression of the love of God and the patient endurance that comes from Christ.

2 Thessalonians 3:5
New Living Translation

We live in challenging times full of situations that are beyond our control or understanding. Because of that, we often time rely on what we know, and just try figuring it out on our own. To be in law enforcement, the military, or a first responder during these times can add even more pressure to us when we face situations that are hard to explain, or when we try to search for some kind of understanding. Paul encourages us instead to not rely on our own understanding but to have strength and steadfastness in Christ. God is where true understanding for our lives comes from. We just need to trust in God's love, HIS plan, and be patient with HIS timing.

During the time Paul wrote this, the people of Thessalonica faced many trials and extreme persecution because of their faith. Nothing has changed since then, and we continue to still see these trials and oppositions today. However, Christ was their example for facing the trials and life ambushes with strength, patience, and endurance. Christ is alive today and is still our example when we meet similar trials and life ambushes. We just need to choose to let God lead us and strengthen us like the Thessalonians.

My take away for you is to be strengthened by God's love for you and trust fully in HIM today. John 15:13 says: *There is no greater love than to lay down one's life for one's friends.* Christ willingly laid his life down for us so we could be redeemed, which was God's ultimate expression of love for us.

11 We also pray that you will be strengthened with all his glorious power so you will have all the endurance and patience you need. May you be filled with joy, **12** always thanking the Father. He has enabled you to share in the inheritance that belongs to his people, who live in the light.

Colossians 1:11-12
New Living Translation

Regardless of your background, agency, or occupation, all of us have been in situations where we need to be strengthened and given encouragement. All of us have had our earthly joy taken from us at one time or another, and we have all felt the adversity in this line of work. One thing about joy is we sometimes have a false sense of what it really is. We find earthly joy in people, possessions, places, and situations. However the "joy" that is discussed here is not earthly joy. There are no words that can actually describe real joy. Real joy comes from and is the very nature of God. This is one reason why we should always be thankful for God's goodness and for everything that HE gives us. Additionally, part of this real joy is the joy found in our brothers and sisters of faith. God enables us to share our faith with our brothers and sisters in Christ. We should be willing to pray for them, lift them up, and strengthen them in their Christian walk. Likewise, we should be always willing to pray for our brothers and sisters in the field too, even if they are not believers. We should always be willing to share our faith with others.

My prayer for you today is for physical, mental, and spiritual health, and for real joy from knowing our LORD and Savior Jesus Christ.

God is our refuge and strength,
always ready to help in times of trouble.

Psalm 46:1
New Living Translation

When we look across our careers in law enforcement, the military, or as a first responder, there have been times where we all have been in need of help. It could have been on a call, an operation, or just the day-to-day "routine" work. When our brothers and sisters help us out in one of these situations, we are thankful for them and their help. I have been there and know you have been too. One of these situations I have remembered from being a kid was from my dad. When I was growing in Kansas, we lived near an Air Force Base that had F-4 Phantom aircraft stationed there. Anytime we were outside and saw one flying, my dad would say "Man I love those planes." Being a young boy at the time, and not knowing any different, I asked him one day why he always said that when we saw an F-4. He told me about how he was a radio operator in Vietnam, and they would be in intense firefights or ambushes, and he would call in air strikes from F-4 pilots for help. Those guy would bail them out of the intense situation that they were in, which ultimately helped save their lives on the ground.

Our LORD and SAVIOR Jesus Christ works the same way for us. HE is our protector, our support, and our strength to keep fighting. HE is always here for us whether we are in times of trouble or times of happiness. It is through Christ's sacrifice to help God, that we have ultimately have been bailed out, saved, and redeemed by God our Father. Thanks be to God.

21 Don't you remember that our ancestor Abraham was shown to be right with God by his actions when he offered his son Isaac on the altar? 22 You see, his faith and his actions worked together. His actions made his faith complete. 23 And so it happened just as the Scriptures say: "Abraham believed God, and God counted him as righteous because of his faith." He was even called the friend of God.

James 2:21-23
New Living Translation

When we look across our lives and examine where we are today, most of us will notice a one common theme. We have worked extremely hard to get where we are. As believers in Christ, God wants us to work hard and accomplish successes for HIM and HIS Kingdom too. Sometimes though, we find ourselves in an uphill battle of listening to the worldly external voices around us or getting caught up with the traps of the world instead of living the lives God designed for us to have. Simply put, our words and actions do not line up with our Christian faith.

Abraham was a man that was aligned with God physically, mentally, and spiritually. His unwavering Godly character, his faith, and his actions worked in unison, which made his faith complete, and God found him righteous.

As Christian men and women, we should strive to be more like Abraham and live our lives in alignment with our faith, with our actions, and with the work we do as we serve our communities and nation. My takeaway for today is for you to be strengthened in your relationship with Christ. Strive to live in complete faith like Abraham did and be called a friend of God.

17 Put on salvation as your helmet, and take the sword of the Spirit, which is the word of God.**18** Pray in the Spirit at all times and on every occasion. Stay alert and be persistent in your prayers for all believers everywhere.

Ephesians 6:17-18
New Living Translation

One thing I do before each time I go on duty is complete a final quick equipment check. This includes checking over my primary firearms, ammo, my patrol ballistic vest, heavy rifle vest, and spark testing my TAZER. Then when I leave my driveway, I try to remain mentally focused on the situations going on around me and to try not to let my guard down. In our Christian walk, we should be completing a final check of faith and reflecting on our relationship with God every day like we do when we go on duty. The reflection of our faith can be as simple as checking to make sure we have the necessary PPE to keep us safe, or that our magazine is seated and there is a round in the chamber in our duty weapon. Paul encourages us to put on and wear our salvation daily, just like we wear our body armor. To pick up and spend time in the Word of God, like we would do with our duty weapons when we are training. To be energized men and women of prayer over everything around us, like our TASER energizes the air around it when we spark test it. Then finally, to stay alert in our faith like we should be alert to our surroundings.

My encouragement to you today is be men and women of prayer, pick up and wear your salvation only found through Christ, and spend a set amount of time in the Word of God daily.

10 Create in me a clean heart, O God. Renew a loyal spirit within me.

11 Do not banish me from your presence, and don't take your Holy Spirit from me.

12 Restore to me the joy of your salvation, and make me willing to obey you.

Psalm 51:10-12
New Living Translation

This is a prayer that I have modeled after David for my own walk with Christ. Even though David was a great king, warrior, and man described as a man after God's own heart; he still sinned against God. Regardless of what professions we are in, or how we conduct ourselves off duty, we all have still sinned against God and need redemption. David acknowledged this in his own life after he had an affair with Bathsheba, covered the affair up by creating a murderous plan for her husband Uriah, having him killed in battle, and continuing to rebel against God through his own desires. While we probably have never sinned against God in the same way David did, our hearts can be just as corrupt. Jesus said, *"A good person produces good things from the treasury of a good heart, and an evil person produces evil things from the treasury of an evil heart. What you say flows from what is in your heart."* (ref. Luke 6:45) To do this we need to have the mindset of David and be strengthened as we seek God's presence and forgiveness in our lives.

My take away for you today is to build up a clean heart like David through the salvation found in Christ. Be redeemed and joyfully produce good things for God's Kingdom as you continue to pursue your faith and serve Christ.

11 For I know the plans I have for you," says the Lord. "They are plans for good and not for disaster, to give you a future and a hope. 12 In those days when you pray, I will listen. 13 If you look for me wholeheartedly, you will find me.

Jeremiah 29:11-13
New Living Translation

Working in our line of work can be extremely difficult sometimes. There are the ongoing pressures we endure as we uphold our duty and serve our nation and our communities in a world that increasingly does not like us or what we do a lot of the time. Then there are the personal internal stresses of compartmentalizing what we see and have to do in the line of duty. It can be overwhelming to say the least and hard to explain to those who do not understand. In those times, however, we need to still search for comfort, peace, and some time off to refocus.

Our spiritual lives can have the same situations just as challenging as the situations we face in our work-life. On the surface they can be different, but often times, we just don't like what is going on and want to give up or we simply want for God to fix the situation right now. I have been there and have prayed for God to fix the situation now, in my timing. However, we must remember that God never leaves us, and has a plan for our lives, and that HE only can work in order to prosper us, to give us hope, and to give us a future with HIM. These truths should be a huge comfort to us and give us strength.

My take away for today is to be strengthened when you face difficult situations. Call upon and pray to Christ. HE will listen to you and provide every one of your needs.

16 Now may our Lord Jesus Christ himself and God our Father, who loved us and by his grace gave us eternal comfort and a wonderful hope, **17** comfort you and strengthen you in every good thing you do and say.

2 Thessalonians 2:16-17
New Living Translation

Every single one of us have picked a career to better ourselves and better our communities, or our nation as a whole. On one level or another we all strive to make a difference both personally and professionally while trying to do good works for the people we serve. Often times, however, we see or deal with some of the worst, heart-shattering things people go through in life. Because of the things we see or have to do, we often times try to cope with them, by absorbing them, visualizing them, or trying to compartmentalize them so we can continue the good fight. Way too often this is much harder said than done, and those events can eat at us sometimes on a daily basis dismantling our hope, our dreams, or causing us to completely shutdown or lose sight of the things important to us like our families, friends, and careers.

As believers in Christ, we need to let God's love for us help us in those times. Our hope should not come from the things of this life, but should come from God's abounding love and grace for us. When we find ourselves losing sight of what is true or struggling professionally, personally, or spiritually, we need to dig deeper into our relationship with Christ. By doing so, we let God form us and be our strength and our comfort so that we can continue doing good in everything we say and do for HIS everlasting kingdom.

You are my strength; I wait for you to rescue me,
for you, O God, are my fortress.

Psalm 59:9
New Living Translation

Throughout our careers there have been times that we have been placed in situations that are potentially dangerous, or life threatening. Regardless of what agency or military branch you are with, we have all been in that place. There are probably situations that comes to your mind right now too. One situation that stands out in my mind, is being on a call where we needed to arrest an individual with felony warrants who was known to have a history of shooting at cops. Of course we staged off-site, developed a plan, and had multiple officers in place before conducting the operation to apprehend the individual. Our spiritual lives are no different than our physical lives. Like David, we are wise to wait on God in times of danger and difficulty. When we do, God strengthens us, helps us, defends us, and rescues us from physical and spiritual danger. We can look throughout David's life and see the accounts of where God protected him. From his youth and the fight with Goliath, to his time on the run from King Saul who wanted to kill him out of jealousy, to being elevated to King of Israel, and being redeemed by God after he sinned against HIM. All of these attributes of David and his warrior mindset still apply to us today whether we are on duty or not. The God of David's time is the same God today. When we pray out and call on the LORD, HE is there. HE is our strength, our help, our defense, and HE has rescued us from sin through HIS son Jesus.

My take away for you today is be a person of faith like David. Rely on Christ for HIS divine strength, help, and defense physically and spiritually.

9 If you openly declare that Jesus is Lord and believe in your heart that God raised him from the dead, you will be saved. **10** For it is by believing in your heart that you are made right with God, and it is by openly declaring your faith that you are saved. **11** As the Scriptures tell us, "Anyone who trusts in him will never be disgraced."

Romans 10:9-11
New Living Translation

As members of the law enforcement, first responder, and military community, we make critical decisions nearly everyday on or off duty. In the very nature of our line of work, some decisions we make can be a matter of life and death either for us individually, the brothers and sisters we serve with, or the people we interact with on a call, scene, or operation. The reality of that is some of these critical decisions we make can be as simple as wearing your seatbelt or not texting and driving. Unfortunately, as law enforcement and first responders, we have responded to accident scenes where we have seen the repercussions of these decisions, and their consequences.

One of the biggest and most critical physical and spiritual decisions we can make in our lives is answering God's gospel message of salvation. It is by declaring our faith in Jesus Christ and God's grace and love for us that we are saved and redeemed.

My encouragement for you today is if you haven't openly declared with your heart, mind, and soul that Jesus is Lord, do it today. It is the biggest and most important decision you will ever make.

8 Stay alert! Watch out for your great enemy, the devil. He prowls around like a roaring lion, looking for someone to devour. 9 Stand firm against him, and be strong in your faith. Remember that your family of believers all over the world is going through the same kind of suffering you are.

1 Peter 5:8-9
New Living Translation

In our profession, we need to be alert at all times, and our lives could depend on it. We have all seen on the news where law enforcement personnel have been ambushed, shot, and really hurt or killed. It happens across our deployed military community and has even happened in our first responder community. Because of the arena we all work in, we need to be diligent, keep our heads on a swivel, and aware of our surroundings at all times.

Our spiritual walk with Christ is no different than how we operate in the field. The Devil wants to destroy us, our relationships, and our relationship with God. Just like when we are on patrol, as Christian men and women, we need to stay diligent, keep our faith on a swivel, and be aware of our spiritual surroundings at all times.

One way I do this is by spending time in prayer, and in the Bible everyday. Even if it is only five minutes or between calls, spending time with Christ allows me to stand firm, build my faith, and to be strengthened by God.

My take away for you today is stay alert professionally and spiritually. Spend some time with God today, and be strengthened in your faith. Finally, look for ways to strengthen your brothers and sisters in Christ and in the field.

33 God is my strong fortress, and he makes my way perfect.
34 He makes me as surefooted as a deer, enabling me to stand on mountain heights. 35 He trains my hands for battle; he strengthens my arm to draw a bronze bow. 36 You have given me your shield of victory; your help has made me great. 37 You have made a wide path for my feet to keep them from slipping.

2 Samuel 22:33-37
New Living Translation

In our line of work there are times where we face relentless, daunting, and grueling situations. We experience adversities and have challenges that most people will never see in their lifetimes or be able to comprehend. Not to mention the extreme weather conditions or exposures we face, or the long days, nights, and or possibly months we work away from our families, loved ones, and friends. These environmental factors can literally hammer us physically, mentally, and spiritually leaving us drained as we try serve as husbands, wives, fathers, mothers, our communities, our nation, and God.

Whether we are on duty or at home, as believers in Christ, God should be our confidence and hope in these times of adversity. While this can be difficult for us at times, Christ makes our path strait and perfect. We need to have courage, to trust in God's ways, and to be strengthened by HIM in all things. Doing so will enable us to stand on a solid foundation of faith for Christ, HIS righteousness, and the path HE created for us.

My encouragement for you is to make God your fortress, and shield more today than you did yesterday. Stand firm on HIS foundation and be strengthened in the great things Christ has in store for you.

Jesus said: **26** But when the Father sends the Advocate as my representative—that is, the Holy Spirit—he will teach you everything and will remind you of everything I have told you. **27** I am leaving you with a gift—peace of mind and heart. And the peace I give is a gift the world cannot give. So don't be troubled or afraid.

John 14:26-27
New Living Translation

In our line of work knowledge is key. Whether we are community policing our neighborhoods, fighting fires, treating patients, or conducting military operations abroad, we need to be confident in our abilities, and be knowledgeable about what is going on in those particular circumstances in order to be successful. This is one of the reasons we stage off-site before going on a scene and conducting a high-level call or mission.

Our faith in Christ runs parallel with this operator mindset. We are reminded of Jesus' teachings through the indwelling of Christ's free gift of the Holy Spirit and through our time reading and studying the Bible. As believers in Christ, the Holy Spirit lives in us to be our instructor and guide as we pursue and build our faith in Christ. He is our staging area in our faith who provides us with a source of peace and comfort as we operate in this world as Christians and face the life ambushes and challenges.

My encouragement for you today is expand your knowledge of the Word of God through your devotion to God and HIS desires for you. Listen to the Holy Spirit's advice in your life and be strengthened by HIS peace of mind and heart. Shalom.

MONTH THREE: STRENGTH

2 Pray, too, that we will be rescued from wicked and evil people, for not everyone is a believer. **3** But the Lord is faithful; he will strengthen you and guard you from the evil one.

2 Thessalonians 3:2-3
New Living Translation

It doesn't take too much of a look in this world to realize that it can be a place full of people absolutely hellbent on hatred, wickedness, and flat out evil in every possible manner. I have seen it, and I know you have too. There are people in our communities, nation, and world that just enjoy hurting other people. The really sad reality is we have seen such an uptick of these people wanting to hurt or kill members of the law enforcement, first responders, and military communities.

This scripture is a prayer that I have said while responding to some of the sketchy calls I have responded to. Just a simple prayer for everyone involved, that we will be able to do jobs efficiently and safely as we conduct business.

However, that prayer I have said multiple times is a prayer on the physical side. As believers in Christ, this is a good prayer to say regarding our faith, and for our brothers and sisters in Christ. We need to constantly remember that we are in a spiritual war too. A war against the Devil's schemes, who wants to hurt and kill us spiritually and keep us from the men and women that God has called us to be.

My encouragement to you today is remember that God is faithful in HIS promises to us. Lean on HIM for strength and protection physically, mentally, and spiritually.

The Lord is for me, so I will have no fear.
What can mere people do to me?

Psalm 118:6
New Living Translation

Everywhere we look in our society today there is something that we can find to be afraid of that keeps us from moving forward. Our past failures, viruses, diseases, and people that professionally and spiritually hate us because of our occupations and faith are just a few.

When we look at David's life, his life had many similarities to our lives today. David had failures, sinned against God, and had setbacks in life. However, one thing that sometimes sets David apart from us is he always put God first in his life. Because of his life-long devotion to the LORD, God was on his side, blessed him, fought his battles, and gave him victories over his enemies even from a very young age. Our walk with Christ should not be any different from David's walk with the LORD. First of all, we need to put God in control of our lives on a daily basis and have a warrior's faith. Additionally, we need use that warrior's faith to model ourselves after David's love for God, and realize that God is our helper, our defender, and we should not be afraid of anything in this life when we are walking with Christ. God's power is simply mightier than anything that we might face in this life, and there is nothing in this world that can remove Christ's love for us.

My desire for you today is to set yourself apart from the world and be a Godly warrior of faith like David. Continue to put Christ in the center of your life, and live fearlessly for the LORD.

Forward Observation: _____

_____

_____

_____

_____

_____

_____

_____

_____

_____

_____

_____

_____

_____

_____

_____

_____

_____

_____

_____

_____

Forward Observation: _____

_____

_____

_____

_____

_____

_____

_____

_____

_____

_____

_____

_____

_____

_____

_____

_____

_____

_____

_____

_____

_____

Forward Observation: _____

_____

_____

_____

_____

_____

_____

_____

_____

_____

_____

_____

_____

_____

_____

_____

_____

_____

_____

_____

_____

Forward Observation: _____

_____

_____

_____

_____

_____

_____

_____

_____

_____

_____

_____

_____

_____

_____

_____

_____

_____

_____

_____

Forward Observation: _____

_____

_____

_____

_____

_____

_____

_____

_____

_____

_____

_____

_____

_____

_____

_____

_____

_____

_____

_____

_____

_____

Forward Observation: _____

_____

_____

_____

_____

_____

_____

_____

_____

_____

_____

_____

_____

_____

_____

_____

_____

_____

_____

_____

_____

ACKNOWLEDGMENTS:

I am grateful for my dad. Not only is he a Vietnam War Veteran and former law enforcement officer, he is more importantly a man of faith. He lead our household by a Christian example with my mother while my younger brothers and I were growing up and has shared his faith in Christ with us over the years. Through his example, he taught and showed my brothers and I how to be Christian men.

To my wonderful wife and best friend Brandi, you have always been a solid rock beside me. You have always been a source of support and motivation to me, and pushed me to strive further and harder to pursue my calling in law enforcement. Thank you for also blessing me with our two beautiful kids, and for being a Godly example to us. I am more than blessed to have you in my life and grateful for you and the kids everyday.

Thank you to my dear friend Chaplain Johnson for our weekly Bible studies, spiritual encouragement, and for being a sounding board throughout the writing of this devotional. I want to additionally thank my friends John "Saint Nick" Cassel, Greg Amundson, K. Friday, and B. Garcia for our discussions and the encouragement you gave me throughout designing, writing, and producing of this devotional.

Thank you to my editing team L. Werbner and M. Mauldin for the countless hours of proofreading and editing this devotional to ensure that it is clean and grammatically sound.

Finally, I want to thank everyone who has picked up and taken the time to read this devotional. I am beyond honored to be able to share my faith in Christ with all of you over the past few months. May God's peace and protection be with you everyday.

Made in the USA
Las Vegas, NV
09 December 2023

82403583R00064